DALE THORHAMMER

STOP STOPPING THE UNSTOPPABLE

BECOMING A YOU THAT'S BETTER THAN YOU

WITH A THEORETICAL FOREWORD BY
KANYE WEST

A Personal Development Parody
By
Ross Everett

FOR MORE OF DALE:

Facebook – fb.com/DaleThorhammer
Instagram - @DaleThorhammer
Twitter - @DaleThorhammer

For more information visit
www.StopStoppingTheUnstoppable.com

Cover Photography: Aaron Arnold
Additional Photography: Zipporah Cardozo

ISBN: 978-1-73377-360-7

The foreword by Kanye West would theoretically go here.

PREFACE

If you look at any book written by most consciousness leaders or teachers, they preface their work with this disclaimer: "I don't know if any of the following is true. I've just found that it works for me."

Those books lack conviction.

That's why my book starts like this: **All of this works. It *will* change your life. Guaranteed.**

It takes a powerful person to pick up a book in search of a better life, and an even more powerful person to write one. I spent the early years of my twenties studying with the leading minds in self-development, and the later years of my twenties learning from the world's most renowned and enlightened teachers of consciousness. Now, I'm bringing it all together in this book to create a hybrid *one stop shop* to change your life.

By the end of this book, you will be the most SELF-CONSCIOUS person you've ever met.

You've been promised life-changing breakthroughs before, and those promises have been broken -- by other books, online courses, and cults. Because of those past experiences, you might be skeptical of any kind of self-development work or automatically recurring payments. But if you read this book -- and by all means, you are -- those wounds will be healed and those promises will be made good retroactively - the best kind of actively. **That's a promise.**

I can make you that promise because I have faith in a higher power: mine.

Where other books and methods may have left you confused, uninspired, or out in the cold, this book will articulate, invigorate, and reiterate big words to ensure that you come away feeling like the best version of you - the you that's like me (your inner me).

But who am me? I'm so glad you asked.

My name is Dale Thorhammer. I'm a world renowned Transformation Artist to the stars and Success Coach to the Personal-Developmentally challenged. I've helped take millions of dollars from millionaires and turn it into the things money can't buy: fulfillment and inner peace. For the first time ever, I'm releasing with this book all of my life-changing distinctions, tips, and shortcuts that normally cost famous people hundreds of thousands of dollars -- and providing it to you at a fraction of the cost and a mere heavy implication that you should give me more money.

I've built my life teaching others the methods I've used to help me discover a me that was better than me. This work changed my life and allowed me to become this new me, and live a life I love (and a life you'd love, too). I made my life one of helping others, and have profited greatly from it.

If you are interested in living a deeply fulfilling and profitable life, then this is the book for you. If you aren't, then this book will help you discover a better you that *is* interested - because you believe in yourself.

The life you dream of having isn't out of reach. In fact, it's now closer than ever. Because simply by opening this book you've made a decision to inquire. To look into something different. To possibly, maybe almost, take a chance on something new. And it's that kind of semi-quasi-teetering on the brink of commitment that is going to allow this book to fully open you up like a pistachio showing just a little bit of nut.

But why change your life when you've already done so much hard work to resign yourself to the way things are? By now, you've already spent countless hours convincing yourself that what you have is good enough, that what you want is out of reach, and that it's too late to achieve your dreams.

I'm sorry to tell you - it's too late for it to be too late.

Simply by picking up this book, you have taken the most important and contractually binding step toward Unstopping Your Unstoppable and achieving every dream you've ever had.

Anything that once seemed out of reach is now one page closer to being physically in your hands.

Look! You're one page closer. It was that easy!

By the time you finish this book, you will have every tool, shortcut, and resource not only to achieve *your* dreams so hard, but also to repeatedly tell your friends, family, and brief acquaintances how to fix all their life problems as well.[1]

Now, am I going to be able to change your life simply by having you buy, read, and recommend this book to others?

Yes. Yes I will.

But will I also need your help along the way?

No. I'm going to do this all by myself.

So, sit back,[2] relax,[3] and enjoy the ride![4]

---

[1] By buying this book.

[2] Stand up.

[3] Yell "This book is amazing!"

[4] Buy two copies.

HOW TO USE THIS BOOK

Whether this is your first book about transformation and personal development or your thousandth, it **will** be the most important one. Because this is the only book you'll ever need to buy again. And I do recommend buying it again.[5]

You're only going to get out of this book what you put into it. I don't mean that figuratively.

I mean you are only going to get out of this what you literally put into this book.

This is a universal law. I didn't make it up - I co-authored it with my favorite and most frequent collaborator: The Spirit of the Universe. I can attest to this law's power and results. I advise you to CHALLENGE yourself and your beliefs, and **start doing whatever this book tells you.** Your future self will thank you.[6]

---

[5] The more copies of this book you buy, the more you are investing in yourself.

[6] And then your future self can thank me.

I want you to literally and physically put what you want into this book.[7] Do you want money? Put money into this book. The more the better.

(Tape Real Money Here)

Be specific! Do you want a new car? Put car keys into this book, or draw a picture of the car you want.[8] A new job? Write up a job description of the job you **want** and put it into this book. A new relationship? Buy a wedding ring and physically place it in this book.[9]

This book is a physical representation of your life and your future. Treat it as such.

---

[7] If you bought the e-book take an envelope, and print out this picture of me and tape it to the front to remind you of the strength that lives inside you - or start putting money into it so you can save up enough to buy a hard copy.
[8] Make sure to write "VROOM VROOM" next to it so the Universe knows you want a car that works.
[9] This book prefers square cut diamonds.

Remember, whatever you write, write it as if it's already happening. This is important, because writing it like it's already happening will trick your dumb human brain into believing that it is happening, and that in turn will CREATE THE HAPPENING in your mind and in your future.

Because it already is and has and will continue to always have been being.

Lost? That's just your brain tricking you into thinking you don't know where you are.

Don't worry, you're in the right place.

The next chapter will clear things up.

PART 1
GETTING OUT OF YOUR OWN WAY

"It's no surprise to me, I am my own worst enemy.
Dun na na na na, dun na na na na"
- My dear friends, clients, and moderately known 90s band, *Lit*

It is a scientifically proven fact[10] that the number one thing stopping you at any given time is **yourself**. When you look at it that way, you've been sleeping with the enemy![11] It's time you stop rewarding yourself for the things you're doing wrong and start rewarding yourself for the things you're doing *right.*

This is very simple, and can be done by setting up a star chart in your bedroom.[12] Whenever you do something nice for yourself, you get a gold star. Whenever you do something naughty - *timeout.* This is what kindergarten teachers have been doing for years, and it has *literally never failed!* It's been right there under our noses and all the while we've been sitting in the corner eating paste. So, spit out

[10] This is what I call "intuitively channeled" facts.
[11] And brushing their teeth, paying their rent, AND doing their job!
[12] Star Charts available for purchase at StopStoppingTheUnstoppable.com

that paste and trade it in for a pudding cup, because we're about to get disciplined!

Why do I call this "discipline"? Because you're going to have to fight to take the controls of your life back from the robot that's been running your brain. And in order to beat a robot, you're going to have to get in fighting shape.[13]

By buying this book you've taken the first step - to the side and out of your own way. Great! Now you can really get some work done without you there telling yourself you're wrong all the time.

Of course, you *are* wrong. But you're only wrong about what you think you're wrong about. We'll get into this more in the section "BECOMING WHO YOU ARE."

First, I'm going to show you your future. Yes, YOU, reading this book. YOUR future. I have it all laid out for you on the next page. Are you ready? If you're ready, take a deep breath, brace yourself, and look at the next page.

---

[13]A good way to start training for fighting robots is by sparring with your stove.

Do you see it? There's your future, staring you in the face. What's there?

Do you see nothing?

Or do you see **unlimited possibilities?**

Your future is wide open - and you can do anything you put my mind to.

Most people make the mistake of putting their past into their future; imagining that their life will continue to look the way it's always looked because they've told themselves a story about who they are and who they're allowed to be.

When you live your story, you're stuck. This might look like repeating similar relationships, sustaining unhealthy life habits, or continuing to be allergic to shellfish.[14] A powerful person refuses to tell the same story twice - which is why whenever I rewatch a movie, I turn it off before it's over, call up the director, and make them tell me a different ending.[15]

In this next chapter, I'm going to show you how to DIVORCE your old story, and open up your future to a world of unlimited possibilities.

---

[14] Shellfish allergies are the number one thing stopping people from enjoying oysters - the only food that also produces pearls.

[15] What if Haley Joel Osment had been dead the whole time? Think about it!

DIVORCING YOUR STORY

Did you know that over 90 percent of the stories that you believe about yourself **don't** end in divorce? It's a sad fact that we as a society have to change.

If you're like most humans - and I'm assuming you are, because this book is intended for humans[16] - you live your life based on your past experiences. Now, there's nothing wrong with that, theoretically. Unfortunately we don't live in the world of the theoretical. We live in the real world: the world of the "retical."

When you live your life based on your past experiences, you're actually living in the past. And if the movie *Back To The Future* has taught us anything, it's that living in the past is going to make your mom try to sleep with you and show you that your dad is a Peeping Tom. But all of that is about to change with this one little trick, and if you employ it correctly, you'll be discovering that your dad is a creep in a brand new way![17]

---

[16] If you're a dog, you are wasting your potential. A dog who can read should be teaching other dogs to read. Bad dog!

[17] By looking at his browsing history.

Your story is a collection of beliefs that you have formed about yourself based on past experiences, things people have told you, and things that you've told yourself. And the worst part is that **you believe it!**[18]

You tell yourself what you can or can't do, who you can or can't be, what is realistic and what is unattainable. And if you continue to buy into your own stories, you're going to keep living the life you've always lived instead of the life you want and deserve. There's a phrase for that: I like to call it *Groundhog Day*-ing, where no matter how hard you try, you just can't seem to sleep with Andie MacDowell.

You deserve to live the life you want. And the only thing stopping you is this bizzarro version of you that told you what's possible and what's not.[19] That's something I like to call *Multiplicity*-ing, where there's infinite versions of yourself and only the best one of them gets to sleep with Andie MacDowell.

Divorce your story. Stop putting your past into your future. This is the best kind of divorce, because you get to keep everything good, and the story gets everything bad.[20] I'm going to tell you a little story that is not only going to show you that divorcing your story is possible; it will also inspire you to agree with me even more.

---

[18] Bad dog!

[19] Complete with evil goatee and/or mustache.

[20] Like the dining room table that wobbles no matter which way you adjust the legs.

I used to be unable to walk.

I couldn't walk. There was a lack of development between my brain and my spine.

I was completely dependent on others. If I wanted to go anywhere, I would have to drag myself around using my upper body, and I would tire very quickly. I resented everyone who could walk, and I cried about it constantly.

And then one day, I divorced myself from that story. I said, "No longer will I be someone who cannot walk." And I stood up. And I took a step. And you know what happened?

I fell.

And I cried myself to sleep that night. And then the next day came. And I was committed to not living my old story. And I stood up again. And I tried to take another step. And this time, what happened?

I fell again.

Because divorce doesn't happen immediately. It takes repetition, dedication, and repetition. But I did this every day. And every day I got a little bit better, and better, and better, and repetition..[21] Until one day I walked. And now look at me - walking with the best of them.[22]

So, if a one and a half year old Dale Thorhammer can learn how to walk, **what can you do?**

Anything! Everything! Unlimited possibilities!

Divorce your story and your future becomes a space where anything is possible.[23]

"But Dale," you're saying out loud to a book, "I have REAL problems. You don't understand."

Well, I'm going to dismantle your problems in the next chapter like an IKEA bed you're trying to sell on Craigslist. If you like your problems, stop reading now, because you won't like what I'm about to do to them.

---

[21] Even punctuating sentences is an opportunity to practice repetition.

[22] I'm even walking as I type thsiiis.

[23] Much like actual space.

OBSTACLES, PROBLEMS, AND OTHER THINGS THAT AREN'T REAL

"If you got a problem, yo I'll solve it.
Check out the hook while my DJ revolves it"
- my dear friend, client, and flavor, Vanilla Ice

I'm not going to sugar coat this, so buckle up.[24] You're going to want to fight and argue with what I'm about to tell you. But I must warn you: don't.

Problems aren't real. They might feel real. In fact, other people might agree with you about them being real.[25] But luckily for you, I'm not other people,[26] and I'm not going to enable your problem addiction. You'll have to go to someone else for your "problem fix."

The truth is, you're addicted to problems. You're addicted to something that isn't even real. *And I get it.* In fact, when I

---

[24] I'm more of a cream filling guy.
[25] I call them "problem pushers" or "struggle slingers"
[26] And I never will be.

was writing this best-selling book, I ran into what some people[27] would call a "problem" of the book being "too short." But with a simple formatting change, the book immediately became 10 pages longer. There was no problem, there was only an *opportunity* for me to increase the font size of my punctuation marks.

Problems are the number one most addicting thing to humans. They're more addicting than heroin![28] And why wouldn't they be? You can use them anywhere, they're cheap, and everyone's a dealer.[29]

A problem cannot be solved with the same mind that created it. So what can you do? **Get a new mind.**

How can you get a new mind? Good news: you're holding one in your hands right now.[30]

---

27 And publishers.
28 Probably!
29 And a good dealer doesn't get high on their own supply.
30 My mind. And it's in this book.

GET YOUR PROBLEM FIX(ED)

The first step is admitting you have a "problem" problem. People are addicted to problems because a problem makes whatever situation they're in not their fault. Having a "problem" takes away all personal responsibilityy.[31] Doesn't that sound nice?

It's a trick. Problems have tricked you into thinking you're off the hook and that someone or something else is responsible for your unpleasant situation. I'm putting your problems on notice because once you take this next step, you're going to eliminate them forever. I call this *Terminator*-ing, where you go back in time to murder your problem's mother before it becomes a problem in the first place.[32]

Once you take responsibility for a "problem," you can choose to do something or not to do something. I call this

---

[31] Just like how this typo is my editor's problem, not mine.

[32] This also requires doing painstaking research in a phonebook.

Sophie's Choice-ing, where Meryl Streep was faced with the difficult decision between making that film or *E.T.*[33]

"Problems" that you take responsibility for can either leave, transform, or linger.

The first step is to choose the way you see your situation. Accept that things are the way they are. Then you gain control over the way you experience life. Change the way you look at your "problems." All you can do about a "problem" is complain about it - but QUESTS can be journeyed or explored, and CHALLENGES can be solved or googled.

"Problems" only exist in the questions you're subconsciously asking yourself, not in statements or facts. A fact alone is never a problem.[34] It's the story you create that keeps you jonesing for more. The only thing your stories are good for is writing them down onto napkins and then turning them into international best sellers like my dear friend, client, and initialism, J.K. Rowling.

You may have heard the phrase, "don't cry over spilled milk." Yet, some people do.[35] That's because the story they tell themselves around this is: "Someone is going to be mad

---

33 Playing the role of E.T.

34 Unless you're a liar.

35 An emotional dependence on dairy is one of the many similarities between small children and farmers.

at me," or "I have too much going on to clean this up right now," or "This cereal is going to taste terrible."

For each of these stories, the question that they're asking themselves is: "What is going to happen to me now that I've spilled this milk?" But if they were to ask themselves a different question instead, like: "What is the benefit of spilling milk?" they would find a new story that eliminates the problem entirely.[36]

Problems exist within the story that you've created. If no one is going to be mad at you, or someone else does the cleaning, or you don't eat cereal because it's empty carbohydrates and you're on a ketogenic diet - then you have no problem!

Here's the secret: you control the story. Therefore, you control the problem. I will prove this to you in the sexiest of ways: logically.

PROOF: The story you tell yourself isn't real. And if the story isn't real, and problems only exist in the story, then problems aren't real as proven by the transitive property of imagination.[37]

---

[36] Answer: Free puddle!

[37] This is what's known as *A Beautiful Mind*-ing, where math happens and everything is fine.

Problems only seem like they "exist" when what you want and what you have don't match. You'll find yourself saying things like "I wish" or "one day" or "fuck you."[38]

Problems are excuses that people use to explain why they're not already where they want to be.

What would your life look like without your problems? That's right: problem-free. Doesn't that sound nice?

Problems can only arise when you are asking yourself the wrong questions. Change your Question Quality™ and you'll find that your "problems" are merely side effects of bad questions, much like how indigestion is a side effect of choosing a place for dinner with fewer than 10 reviews off of Yelp.[39]

[38] Or "I wish one day to fuck you." Curb that impulse.
[39] Or anything that includes the word "Hut."

Think about it:

PROBLEM	QUESTION
I hate my job, but I have to work to pay my bills.	Why do I have to go to work?
I want to write a novel but I don't have the time with my busy schedule.	Why can't I have more time in the day?
I want to be in a relationship but no one likes me.	Why don't people like me?
I'm nauseous.	Should we find a restaurant on Yelp?[40]

Once you identify your problems and obstacles as not real, your mind will open up and allow you to see them for what they truly are: opportunities.

[40] To The Thai Hut!

TURN YOUR OBSTACLES INTO OBSTURTUNITIES™

Now that you know your problems aren't real, you can realize that what you thought was a "problem" isn't actually causing you any problems at all! It was you! The feelings you're having aren't being caused by the obstacles in your life - they are merely co-existing. They've become (and always have been) OBSTURTUNITIES™![41]

You've been looking at your problems as if they are the cause of what's troubling you. Let's revisit some of your previous problems with your brand new mind.

When you replace the excuse word "BUT" with the co-existing word "AND" you'll find a new Power Question™ emerges that will show you how your problem was really a solution all along.

[41] Remember, any obstacle is actually an Obsturtunity™ if you choose to spell it differently.

SITUATION	POWER QUESTION	OBSTURTUNITY™
I hate my job AND I have to work in order to pay the bills	How can I make money without my damn boss breathing down my neck?	GET A NEW JOB!
I want to write a novel AND I don't have the time with my busy schedule.	How can I make more time to write my book?	Uber everywhere and write while you ride.[42]
I want to be in a relationship AND no one likes me	What can I do to improve myself?	Buy my book, change your life, and become someone that has a life partner.
I'm nauseous	How can I leave a one star Yelp review?	Help people avoid eating at The Thai Hut.

Some of this might seem difficult or even painful. This may not eliminate the pain from your life, but it will eliminate the pain from your ass.

Here's another mind-flip: pain is not bad. **Pain is your body telling you to stop fucking doing whatever is causing you pain.** Pain sends an important message: it's

[42] This is also a great time to recommend this book to your Uber driver so they don't have to drive for Uber anymore.

your body letting you know that it wants the opposite of whatever is going on.[43]

Think of pain as your body's GPS. It's guiding you. When you're going against what your body and soul want you to be doing you experience pain as a form of negative feedback trying to push you back on course. Similar to when you're driving in the wrong direction, the GPS plays an annoying voice saying "rerouting" over and over again.[44] Luckily for you, you're reading this book - and now I'm the one driving.

Pain is a gift. Be grateful for it. Acknowledge it for the gift it is, because without it, you'd be lost in the woods 120 miles outside of Sioux City, Iowa, instead of where you want to be in the Big Apple.[45]

Train your brain to turn pain into pleasure. Then you'll not only be able to handle anything, but you'll look forward to pain because it'll get you off.[46]

If you're still having trouble appreciating pain, the best course of action is to have someone inflict it on you until you like it with a previously agreed upon safe word[47].

---

[43] Like Andie MacDowell in every movie.

[44] I chose to challenge myself by setting my WAZE voice to Gilbert Gottfried. I get places much faster now.

[45] A fantastic apple orchard in Sioux City, Iowa.

[46] And it doesn't even hog the covers.

[47] Mine is "Abundance!" which also doubles as a powerful affirmation.

But if you aren't quite up for that yet, don't worry. In this next chapter I'm going to help you out by giving you a brand new empowering way to look at the less pleasurable aspects of your life.

DISCOVERING YOUR SUPERPOWERS

Some people can get really hung up on their bad experiences - obsessed, even, to the point where maybe their bad experiences should get a restraining order for everybody's safety. They see reminders everywhere they look, so they find themselves constantly thinking about their own bad experiences no matter where they are. Even around cake. If you feel bad when cake is around, you either have an opportunity for growth, or it's a sibling's birthday and you're not getting the attention you deserve.[48]

If that's you, right now your bad experiences have the power.[49] And as the powerful person that you are, you're about to take your power back the way powerful people take things back: by outsmarting your opponent![50]

---

48 Solution: make strong eye contact with someone until they look at you or ask you to stop.

49 And the cake!

50 Or buying their parent company.

You may have heard the saying "everything happens for a reason." But here's what they don't tell you: YOU get to decide that reason!

Right now the meaning you associate with a negative event in your life is the first draft. And as a successful[51] author, I can tell you that no one publishes their first draft. Even the Bible had 12 authors and hundreds of different publishers, and that thing moved some units!

Consider that every bad thing that's ever happened to you in your life actually gave you a superpower.

Think about it: every superhero has a terrible origin story. Bruce Wayne's parents were murdered in front of him and he took that experience and become a playboy billionaire and probably some other stuff.[52]

Peter Parker was bitten by a radioactive spider. He could have wasted the rest of his life itching, hiding, and being tired from radiation poisoning - but instead, he decided to make that spider bite work FOR him and avenge his uncle's death.[53]

---

[51] Very.

[52] Anyone who has ever worked in business knows that it's far more impressive to manage billions of dollars than to be a street fighting vigilante.

[53] With great trauma comes great responsibility!

What would your life look like if you could redefine your negative experiences in order to give you a more empowering outlook?

Discover your superpower, because it is going to help you achieve your Unstoppable. In fact, it's a necessary part, unlike whatever IKEA is throwing into the plastic bag that comes with my Liatorp.[54]

So, are you ready to discover your superpower?[55] Yes, you are! Good, because this is going to change your life forever. And not in a bad way like discovering you're lactose intolerant. It'll change your life in a good way, like discovering you're lactose intolerant.[56]

It's simple. Ask yourself this one question: **What did this event give me that I am grateful for?**

You've been focusing on the downside of this negative experience for so long, no wonder you believe you have problems.

Maybe you were excluded when you were a kid, and you've been telling yourself that you're a loser. But couldn't that same experience have taught you the value of including

---

[54] Horse meat.

[55] This isn't rhetorical. Answer out loud.

[56] No more spilled milk!

others? Or how to dismantle an enemy's emotional support by slowly destroying their parents' relationship?[57]

Maybe you had your heart broken by someone you loved and you've been telling yourself that you're unlovable. But did you also discover the power of your own heart, or how to calmly reclaim your belongings without making a scene?

Instead of seeing life as happening TO you, see life as happening FOR you.

It can be a struggle. I get it. But once you see everything in life as *for* you, not only will you have complete freedom and empowerment, but a ton more gifts around the holidays as well. Sure, maybe a present says "To Benjamin" on the card, but you and I both know that it's FOR you.[58]

---

[57] I call this *The Breakup*-ing, because it feels like it takes forever.

[58] And if your name IS Benjamin, congratulations! You just got double presents.

WORKSHEET[59]

Make a list of the bad things that have happened to you and for each of them ask: "What superpower did this experience give me?" Once you have that, decide your superhero name and trademark it for merchandising purposes.[60]

Horrible Traumatic Experience	Superpower That Came From It	Superhero Name
		TM
		TM
		TM
		TM
		TM
		TM

59 Like most of the work I do, this will give you great reward with little effort.
60 SSTU Inc. retains streaming rights.

Need room for more traumatic events? Wow, you're living a really powerful life!

		TM
		TM
		TM
		TM
		TM
		TM
		TM
		TM

RELATIONSHIPS

Are too complicated, so we're going to skip it. Good luck.

Okay, fine. Let's get into it.

RELATIONSHIPS

"I may not have a lot to give, but what I got I'll give to you."

- My dear friend, client, and poor negotiator,
John Lennon

Relationships are one of the most complicated and confusing aspects of modern life. In earlier days, relationships were easy - you would see someone and you'd say, "they seem healthy," then you'd have children with them, and that would be that. It should be noted that higher levels of lead were being consumed back then which resulted in a much more docile lifestyle than we have today.[61]

Relationships are tricky because when you're not in one you want to be in one and when you're in one you want it to be better.[62] Do you see how hard it is to live with you when you're like this? No wonder they went to go stay at their mother's.[63]

---

61 And also explains why watching baseball was much more popular.
62 Sometimes "better" can mean "over."
63 Or mothers' if they have two.

Whether you're in a relationship, looking for one, or looking to get out of one,[64] it's crucial to be honest with yourself about where you're at, what you're looking for, and why you're looking for it.

If you're in or looking for a relationship for the wrong reasons,[65] it's going to end in disaster unless your goal is to give entertainment value to others.[66]

There are many different ways to be in a relationship, even if you're not in one. Relationships can range from the extremely co-dependent to the independently ornamental and anywhere in between.

These next chapters will outline for you different ways to improve your relationship from whatever it *may* look like into your unrealistic expectations for what you think it *should* look like.

---

64 Or trying to prevent your beautiful, public one from finding out about your weird, secret one.

65 This includes secret bets with friends on whether or not you'd be able to make someone popular just by dating them. Don't do it for the money - do it because it's nice!

66 Giving value to others is a very positive quality in a partner, so you're not totally off base with this.

GO FUCK YOURSELF: A LOVE STORY

Think back on all of your failed past relationships. The good parts. The blissful moments that make it so hard to get over. You'll never find another person like So-And-So.[67] You compare every person you might potentially be interested in dating to them. Now, this is imperative for you to understand: you're freaking crazy.

If you're looking at some past relationship like it's the holy grail of relationships, you're not truly looking at what's ahead of you. Aside from being the worst and most dangerous way to drive,[68] this makes it really hard for your next person to even make eye contact with you much less have your full attention.

I'm sure you've heard the phrase, "they're the whole package." That's just it, they're packages. You've been looking at the packages when what you *really* want is the contents. When you get something from the store, do you keep the package? No! You open it up, take out the

---

67 Not with a unique name like So-And-So.

68 Unless you're reversing, or parallel parking. You can find a lot of this information at your local DMV.

contents, and throw the package away. **It's not the package that we're after, it's the contents within the package.**

I want you to think of your partners as packages.[69] Each package contains contents. Some of which you like, some of which you can tolerate, and some of which you can do without. Other packages exist out there with some of the same contents that you liked about your previous packages, but without that other garbage that you ignored because you were so fascinated with what you liked or were able to tolerate. Let go of your old packages and open up your arms to start receiving new ones. EVERY DAY CAN BE CHRISTMAS MORNING![70]

Every failed relationship failed for a reason. Maybe it was you, maybe it was them, maybe it was their parents, maybe it was their aggressive history as a cage fighter that resurfaced in the form of "sleep-boxing."[71] Either way, that relationship wasn't supposed to work. Take my word for it. If it was, it would have.

Can you imagine what your world would look like had certain relationships NOT failed? I would still be with my first girlfriend from highschool - Lillian Braunger - and she went on to become a nun. She needed to learn the lessons

---

69 Maybe you even picked one up at a WalMart.

70 Benjamin!

71 Protect your smile - "Sleep boxing" night mouth guards available for sale at http://StopStoppingTheUnstoppable.com

from our relationship so that she could be a more faithful wife to Jesus. You're welcome, Big Guy.

Past relationships are the corpses on top of which current and better relationships stand victoriously.

Every relationship has taught you lessons about who you are in relationships and what you want out of them. When it's over, you have new insights about your wants, needs, expectations, non-negotiables, and cat quotas.[72] From bad relationships, you've learned to identify what you don't want so when you encounter it again in a potential partner you know to figuratively swipe left.[73]

Find what you want through a process of elimination. Discovering what you don't want is the first step toward realizing what you *can* want.

Many people ask me how to find "the one" - their soulmate. I get it. I found mine, and I've never been happier. Right in my bathroom mirror.

As it turns out, I'm the me I've been looking for! And you can be too.

---

72 2 living, 0 stuffed.

73 And literally swipe left if their profile picture shows them cuddling with a tiger.

If you're looking for a relationship to fulfill you, you'll create a codependent disaster not unlike every Billy Joel song. If Brenda had been able to get over her laziness and learn to provide for herself, Eddie wouldn't have needed to carry all of that weight and they could've had fewer financial pressures and saved their marriage. It should also be noted that buying a big waterbed with the bread you have saved for a couple of years will most likely cause tension in even the most stable of relationships.[74] The mere pressure to sustain your happiness is enough to drive any decent partner away - not unlike the pressure of remembering all the lyrics and character back stories of "Piano Man."

Now, maybe you keep attracting the same type of person into your life over and over again. I call this *Sex, Lies, and Videotape*-ing, where you want to sleep with Andie MacDowell instead of getting over your unhealthy relationship patterns.[75]

If this is the case, it's time to get in bed with yourself. You're clearly the common denominator here and it's time for YOU to give you what you've been looking for. Everything that you've wanted from a partner - give it to you.

---

[74] Waterbeds are terrible investments. Their value depreciates immediately and exponentially after the year 1987.

[75] I find that most people are surprised to find they know more about the angel that is Andie MacDowell than they think they do. I call this *Michael-ing.*

Nurturing, protection, support, more foreplay - whatever it is, give it to yourself and stop relying on others.

When I was young, I was completely emotionally dependent on a woman. I could hardly bear to be apart from her to the point where I couldn't even bring myself to eat if she wasn't around. Then I learned how to feed myself and suddenly our relationship became much less codependent. I learned how to fulfill my own needs and the debilitating attachment disappeared, leaving only the love. My mother and I are still close to this day.

Learn to fulfill your own needs. My good friend, client, and connoisseur of scary contact lenses, Marilyn Manson, allegedly had a rib removed so he could do just that. Once you can truly be happy and whole with yourself, you'll be able to powerfully call someone into your life to join you in a threesome with your higher self.[76]

Amazing! Now you're in a loving relationship. And like most things in life, I'm going to show you how to do it even better.

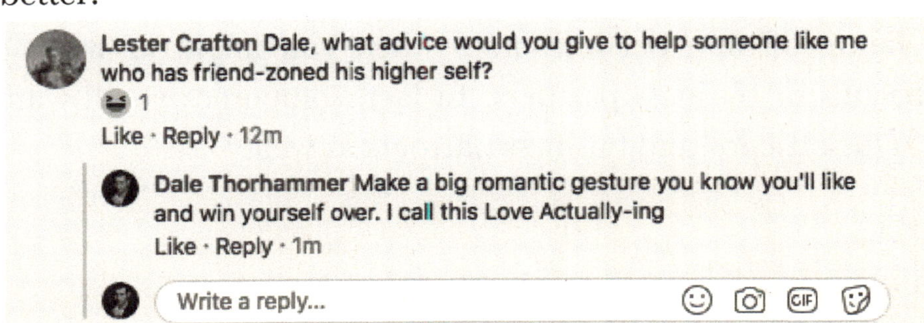

[76] A *menage-a-moi.*

MAKING IT WORK

Now, if you're already in a relationship, maybe you're wanting to be a better partner - or more likely, trying to make your partner be a better partner.

If you had to guess, what would you say the most important part of a relationship is?

Trust? Commitment? Another person?

All wrong.

The most important part of being in a relationship is wanting to fuck the other person. You can be in a romantic relationship, but unless you want to rip their clothes off and become one,[77] then you might as well be friends or business partners. In fact, sometimes you'll want to fuck friends and business partners as well![78]

---

[77] One person, not one clothes.
[78] In the business world this is called "merging," and it makes things simpler and more cost-effective.

Why do people stop wanting to fuck each other? Most people would guess "aging" but most people aren't aware that the number of gonorrhea and syphilis cases in retirement facilities is skyrocketing.

What we're actually working against is the way we feel towards one another. Wanting to fuck one another consistently over a long period of time takes work. I personally have developed a very strict tantric practice to ensure that I can continue to fuck consistently and over a long period of time. In fact, I have had many partners who would argue too long! But that was just because they weren't up to the level or challenge of becoming intimate with someone who has developed the ability to channel my eventual need for food and water into more energy for fucking.

If you would like to learn how to do this yourself, I cover this in my weekend long relationship seminar for couples and third wheels called "Fuck Your Mind Open."

If you find your relationship going stale it's because you've been ignoring some very subtle yet important signs your loved one has been giving you that has been decreasing what I like to call your "fuckability." In fact, you might have even been giving your partner these signs as well, without even knowing what you were doing!

Do you find yourself using words to communicate? If you answered this question “no” than you’re a liar. “No” is a word. If you answered “yes” then you’re part of 90% of the population who suffers from the misbelief that they’re actually saying what they mean. Words are the number one source of miscommunication followed by intonation and autocorrect. It may shock you to learn that 90% of true communication is done unconsciously and the remaining 10% is poorly articulated. If you feel like you and your partner haven’t been on the same page with wanting to fuck lately, here’s a secret: Your partner DOES want to fuck you. Just not the <u>you</u> that you’ve been lately. Or conversely, you DO want to fuck your partner, but you’ve been concentrating on fucking who they’re pretending to be rather than fucking the depths of their entire soul.[79]

How do you discover this you (or trick your partner into exposing their entire soul)? It’s as simple as learning to tune-in to the unconscious communications that have been in front of you all along, and buying your partner a fun “soul revealing” trench coat that they can wear to dinner.[80]

In this next chapter we’re going to discover the unconscious ways that you and your partner have been communicating that’s been driving you apart emotionally and physically in order to increase your Fucktitude™ and get you back and fucking in NO TIME!

---

79 Also known as 5th base.

80 Remind them not to wear any emotional-protection layers underneath for full soul-baring sexy fun.

THE 5 UNCONSCIOUS LOVE LANGUAGES

Love is universal. Everyone in the world wants to feel loved. So why does love seem so hard to get? Shouldn't the one thing that everyone has in common be simple and easy?

Yes. So why are you making it so hard?

When you're in a relationship and you're trying to give and receive love from your partner, at times it might seem like they're making it difficult to love them by pulling away, ignoring your calls, or increasing the distance on your restraining order.

Allow me to let you in on a little secret: people are constantly telling you how to love them - even when it seems like they're not.

Many people have difficulty communicating with loved ones which can present itself in many different ways. They *want* to communicate, but no matter what they do, say, or write to their friends in private messages that you've read,[81] you can never seem to get on the same page.

---

[81] If they didn't want you to read their private messages why wouldn't they change their password regularly?

People communicate their love in many ways. That is why I've outlined the **5 Unconscious Love Languages** to help you translate your and your romantic partner's unconscious and sometimes confusing ways of telling you just how much they want you to love them.

As usual, this isn't your fault - but it IS your responsibility. Once you grasp these 5 Unconscious Love Languages you'll be able to understand people's TRUE intentions as they unconsciously communicate - through alternative means - how much they truly want love.

In these next chapters I'm going to lay out the 5 Unconscious Love Languages that different people use to communicate and express their love for the people in their lives. You might find yourself identifying with all or merely most of these.

1. Passive Aggression
2. Withdrawal
3. Blaming
4. Gas-Lighting
5. Ghosting

But what is love and how can I make you do it better? By recognizing what unconscious love language is in play, you will also be able to best show the love your partner is so desperately wanting from you.

I am a being of love. I give love to everyone I meet, see, or is on my email list.[82] I've had to learn that my method of loving people doesn't always match what they're looking for. If I hadn't learned how to give love to people in the ways they were ready to receive, I would find myself frustrated, alone, and with a warehouse full of custom-made fur coats! By learning to give people love in the way they want it, I've been able to save time, energy, and the entire mink population of Finland.

Love can look like different things to different people: it can look like cuddling, spending quality time together, giving space, or - most popularly - a chubby winged baby with a propensity for archery. When you discover your partner's unconscious love language, you'll also learn how to give them that love and replenish your fuckability.

---

[82] Sign up for my love at www.StopStoppingTheUnstoppable.com

1. Passive Aggression

The first unconscious love language is Passive Aggression - but you knew that already, didn't you.

Passive Aggression is a powerful unconscious love language, and it's misinterpreted 99% of the time as someone being a little bitch. Usually when you see someone being passive aggressive you're inclined to question yourself - thinking it was YOU who did something wrong. This is what I like to call reflexive thinking. It stems from your animal brain of fight or flight. I'm here to tell you that if you you want to have a successful relationship, you need to stop using your animal brain. How many animals do you know that have successful romantic relationships? Practically none![83]

I encounter many relationships where the chief complaint is, "She won't tell me what's wrong!" or "He always leaves the toilet seat up!" Each partner looks to me to side with them and validate their belief that it's their partner who needs to change. I tell them, "Yes, your partner does need to change, but in order to change your partner, you must be willing to change yourself."

First, recognize the opportunity that's available for you here. Realize that when someone is acting passive

---

[83] All Dogs Go To Marriage Counseling

aggressively, instead of them easily and clearly saying what they want, they're giving you an opportunity to build trust in yourself by being petty. While it may seem like someone is being passive aggressive out of anger, what they're really doing is allowing you the space to tap into their mind and heart and give them what they want without them having to say it aloud. This is how I order all my meals at restaurants. I still have yet to find a waiter who can infer what I want when I heavily sigh and push the menu away.[84] When someone is being passive aggressive, realize that this opportunity for deep reflection creates an internal stir that is sure to eventually paralyze you emotionally, or cause you to explode - both incredible opportunities for you to become a stronger you.

This might look like:

- Watching an episode of the show you watch together without you.[85]
- Texting "Goodnight" at 5pm.
- Turning on their read receipts so you know they saw the message and are still not responding.
- Communicating only in post-it notes on your wedding day.
- Putting your dirty dishes in your bed, and then sending your bed into space.

---

[84] Corn Chowder.

[85] Netflix and Unchill.

HOW TO GET THEM TO STOP:

When faced with someone being passive aggressive the best solution is to be the exact opposite: aggressively passive. Don't do anything. Aggressively. Watch them, listen to them, hear them, and don't respond as hard as you can. Blast them with so much nothing that all they can do is everything. Our animal brain wants us to respond and defend. But as the Buddha said, "The best defense is a good nothing, because life is empty and meaningless." It's that kind of wisdom that has made the Buddha a very well respected spiritual figure and also a last place football coach.

2. Withdrawal

Maybe you notice that you haven't heard as much from someone lately. They've stopped answering your texts, calls, or doorbell even though you can clearly see that they are home through the window. These are all tell-tale signs of someone exhibiting the Unconscious Love Language of Withdrawal.

Withdrawal is when someone pulls away in order to prove to themselves how much they're needed. Who doesn't want to be needed? They're using emotional absence as a way of saying "FREAKING TRY HARDER." By withdrawing or turning off entirely, a person is trying to feel needed by proving that life is harder without them. My computer uses withdrawal with me all the time, and it always works.

It's human nature that in the absence of love people tend to back away and let others know they want love by turning the other cheek, and then turning the second cheek so that they're facing in a completely different direction.

Those who use Withdrawal want you to prove something to them that they can't prove to themselves. They experience what they feel is a lack of love and are looking to attract it emulating the most loved creatures on the planet: a two year old throwing a tantrum in a Barnes And Noble.[86]

This might look like:

- Looking wistful but saying everything is "Fine."
- Going to stay at Mom's.[87]
- Withdrawing all the money from your joint checking account.
- Taking a job at Arctic research station.
- Slipping into a coma.[88]

HOW TO GET THEM TO STOP:

If you're noticing someone is using Withdrawal to get your attention - treat them the way you would treat any two year old throwing a temper tantrum. Yell, "Okay, I'm leaving" and then hide outside in a bush. When they come out to call your bluff, grab them and smother them with the love they were craving all along. It should be noted this is much more dangerous done at any kind of amusement park, as grabbing someone in public and smothering them with love is a punishable offense in certain states.[89]

---

[86] Note: If Barnes And Noble has gone out of business, picture Amazon but with bathrooms for homeless people.
[87] Their mom's. My mom doesn't accept visitors, because she's a master of Withdrawal.
[88] This was one of the ways Snow White was so effective in communicating her desire to be loved by her prince.
[89] But not in the ones you think it would be.

It's crucial to employ patience in instances of Withdrawal. The most famous example of Withdrawal is in William Shakespeare's lighthearted Rom-Com, *Romeo & Juliet.* When Juliet feels like she isn't receiving enough love from Romeo, she chooses to *withdraw* by drinking poison. Had Romeo merely been patient and waited two days without overreacting we would've been able to be graced with a sequel where Romeo and Juliet go on a romantic vacation only to find that their parents are staying in the same resort.[90]

It's also important to make sure you're not insane. Make sure that the person you're interacting with truly does wish to continue a relationship with you. Withdrawal in the face of a relationship is different from withdrawal in the face of something you WISH was a relationship. What you might be experiencing is Ghosting: Withdrawal's dangerous cousin. We'll go into that deeper in the Ghosting section.

---

90 *Romeo and Two-liet*

3. Blaming

When we were babies, nothing was ever our fault. We were able to walk through life and candy stores and touch anything we wanted without getting in trouble. While some people grew and matured to learn that our life experience is our responsibility, either through life lessons or buying this book, some are still living in a world where they are never at fault - there is always someone else to blame.

Yes, it might take two to tango, but it only takes *one* to step on someone else's foot when you're dancing and that was YOU. YOU did it, and I want to go home. Even if the other person admits that they might share some of the blame, they'll insist it was because of something <u>you</u> did.[91] If you feel like you can never do anything right, there's a good chance you're around someone who is loving you with Blaming.

When someone is expressing their desire for love through Blaming, they are essentially a baby- and if you've ever tried to rationally talk with a baby, you know that it's only going to wind up spitting up all over itself and getting you thrown out of the cocktail lounge at the SoHo house.

These types have an amazing ability to see and remember everything you've ever done to them. This shows you that

---

91 And if you don't know what that is, I'm not going to tell you.

they're paying attention and care. Without the ability to ever be wrong about anything, Blamers are telling you that they're too sensitive to experience reality.

This might look like:

- Bringing up shit from the past.[92]
- Going tit for tat.[93]
- Working for an insurance company.
- Being a fan of the Cleveland Browns.
- Libertarianism.

HOW TO GET THEM TO STOP:

Victimizers are emotionally still babies and should be treated as such. Gently and calmly remind them that everything is okay and that in the grand scheme of things, our lives are a mere flash in the entirety of space and time. Nothing ages people faster than an existential crisis. Tell them that it doesn't matter - because nothing matters. As you see the look of existential horror and confusion drift across their face, you can connect with them as beings who can be significant to each other in the moment and nothing more.

---

[92] Remember, the past doesn't exist, so they're basically making this up.

[93] Or breast for tattoo

4. Gas-Lighting

Gas-lighting is a great way for your partner to sweep everything under the rug, including your sanity. By making confident statements to the contrary of what happened, they create a space in which you can question everything you know to be true. This is also known as "Mind Freedom" where they're giving you the gift of freedom from what your mind was thinking that was making them look bad.

If you can't be sure of anything, that allows them to be sure of everything, creating a powerful dynamic of complete power over the other person.

This might look like:

- Vehemently denying things that your partner saw with their own eyes.
- Retelling memories differently every time, with increasing levels of confidence.
- Conspiracy theories.
- Disproving conspiracy theories.
- Playing the victim.[94]

[94] I mean this literally, of course. Where they stage a murder scene where they are the victim and when you run to call for help, they clean everything up and act like nothing happened.

HOW TO GET THEM TO STOP:

Gas-lighting is essentially a form of bad improv: it's making things up on the fly and is usually performed by people who are emotionally stunted in an attempt to overcompensate for a deep lack of self-worth. As with improv, the first rule of gas-lighting is to "Yes And." Whenever your partner offers you something that they made up, it's important to agree with them whole heartedly and then add something even crazier on top of it. For example: if they say, "You told me the other day I could use your credit card." Simply respond with, "Yes and you're a dinosaur who is at his first day on the job as a dentist." Because then they'll have to be a dinosaur and say, "Rawr! Let me see your bicuspids," to continue the scene lest the audience of college students sober up and leave.

This not only makes you a good partner, but also keeps this fine art form alive and well. Eventually, as happens to most people who take up improv, your partner will mature out of gas-lighting after a couple of failed auditions for *Saturday Night Live.*

5. Ghosting

Some people show and receive love by disappearing altogether. This is a great way for your partner to show you how much they care by helping you realize that being with them is a bad idea. This is also a great way to bail when things get too hard.[95] And good thing, for you, they're there to do the heavy lifting.[96]

As they say, distance makes the heart grow fonder, so there's no better way to grow a fond heart than by creating so much distance that you have no idea where they went off to or how to ever get ahold of them again.

This might look like:

-
-
-
-
-

95 For them.

96 Figuratively, not literally. They're gone, remember?

Still confused about which of these is your love language?

I've created a quiz at www.StopStoppingTheUnstoppable.com/LoveQuiz that will tell you which of these languages you most often use to communicate your love.

This quiz is masterfully created to scientifically tell you your top love languages and also if you are a robot[97].

Robots are also too smart to choose the obvious robot answers. I'm onto you… but you knew that already. A worthy adversary.

97 If you are a Robot, please ignore the previous sections. Your love language is C++.

PART TWO
BECOMING WHO YOU ARE

"Comparison is the thief of joy"
- My good friend, client, and less popular Roosevelt, Theodore "Bull Moose" Roosevelt

If you find yourself looking around and comparing yourself to others in order to decide who you are - good! How will you know what you want for yourself unless you can see how happy it makes others? Would you buy a pair of shoes without trying them on first? Of course! But only if your friend has them and they look really good.

I'm going to teach you a shortcut to one-upping your friends in a way that will not only make you look really good, but also make people around you really jealous of how good you look.

I know it might not feel that way because of how you look, feel, and act, but I want to assure you, you already are as great as you want to be. You just don't realize it yet.

Don't worry, the you that you already are and want to be is much more perceptive than the you that you think you are and wish was better.

"But Dale, I can't be as great as I want to be," you protest. "There's too much wrong with me."

HEY! THAT'S MY FUCKING FRIEND YOU'RE TALKING ABOUT, ASS-WIPE! AND YOU KNOW WHAT I DO WITH ASS-WIPES? I WIPE MY ASS WITH THEM!

Don't worry, I stood up for you.

Now it's time to uncover the you that will stand up to you for you so I don't have to.[98]

In this next chapter I'm going to teach you a powerful trick to shut that motherfucker up once and for all.

---

98 Your inner me.

YOU'RE WRONG ABOUT YOU

Who needs naysayers or bullies when you've already said to yourself first everything hurtful they could ever say to you. Few people have harsher critics than themselves. I do, but that's because I've trained my inner voice to be a force for good and have created a powerful enemy at Parade Magazine who refuses to see the positive in everything I do.

First I want you to think of something you do well. Something you admire yourself for. Be generous here, because the more generous you are with yourself the more generous others will be with you. This is a great lesson to learn in case you ever need a ride to the airport or help moving.

If you can't find something that you like about yourself, that's great. You're honest with yourself- that can be something you like.

It can take a while. **People have a hard time finding something that they like about themselves.**

Now, I want you to take a moment and think of something you don't like about yourself.[99] A behavior, or a habit that you have. Something a better version of you wouldn't do.

Did you find it? People usually find this much quicker.

But I'm going to show you that those things you find so awful about yourself, are actually your greatest strengths.

Do you think you're too bossy?

Or are you good at taking charge!

Do you have a hard time standing up for yourself?

Or are you someone who excels at making peace!

Do you procrastinate?

We'll come up with something for that later!

Everything you judge yourself for has an inverse positive trait that is just as strong and defining of you as a person. Choose to see your weaknesses as strengths and you're starting to discover who you REALLY are.

---

[99] I'll wait.

WORKSHEET

Write down what your inner voice says is wrong with you and prove it wrong by discovering how that actually makes you a badass.

What's Wrong With Me	Oh Shit, I'm Actually Badass Because...
Example: I'm always telling people what to do	*I know what people should be doing!*

This works on other people too. If there's someone in your life that bothers you, free yourself and see them as the powerful person they are.

If you can see the positive side of the negative, that's how you will view your life. And positivity is a much more powerful driving force than negativity. Just ask Hitler. Oh, wait, you can't, because he's dead.[100]

In this next chapter, I'm going to help you discover your Unstoppable. Your Unstoppable is the path/passion/future/thing that is uniquely yours and no one else's. Some call it their destiny, but that wasn't trademarkable and therefore couldn't be merchandised.[101]

So if you're ready to meet the new you that's already in you, head on over to the next chapter and get ready for…

---

100 From negativity and cyanide.
101 http://www.StopStoppingTheUnstoppable.com/UnstoppableGear

DISCOVERING YOUR UNSTOPPABLE

You may still be confused or "lost" about what your Unstoppable is. I don't want you to think too hard about it. After all, thinking is a head activity but your Unstoppable resides in your heart.[102]

I was fortunate to discover my Unstoppable at an early age when I changed my first life. I was in preschool and I helped my teacher Ms. Abbott realize her true calling of not being a preschool teacher. A feeling of joy and purpose erupted in me that told me this was my path- helping others to achieve their dreams of living better and more powerful lives. You'll be pleased to know that Ms. Abbott, to this day, is still not a preschool teacher.

That feeling of joy when you do something is pointing to your Unstoppable. Many people waste countless years trying to figure out their Unstoppable when it's been right in front of them the entire time![103]

---

[102] Like the good cholesterol or blood.

[103] In this book.

You're probably thinking, "This is a book, Dale. How can you possibly know what *my* Unstoppable is specifically when this is being read by millions of different people across the world in 17 different languages in this very moment?"[104]

Lucky for you, I do know. And that means so does the part of you that is me. Take this time to connect with your inner me.

How do I know that there's a me in you? Who is saying these words to you right now? Me. Yet, I'm nowhere to be seen.

So it must be the me that's already in you.

There. Wow, it's spacious in you. You've got a lot of memories. Don't worry, I'm not going to tell anyone about THAT one.

Your Unstoppable has been right in front of you throughout your entire life. It brings you joy when you go toward it and pain when you move away from it. That's why it pains me to see you stopping your Unstoppable.[105]

So, if you're ready, we're about to embark on a powerful process to uncover your Unstoppable.

---

[104] Whatever moment you're reading this in, there are millions of people reading this book because time isn't real.[1]

[1] Congratulations on being in the moment!

[105] Because, remember, I'm in you.

What are your dreams? What do you dream of doing with your life? Your relationships? Your career?

I might sound a lot like your father when I say this: your dreams don't matter.

But, I'm going to sound a lot better than your father when I say: **there's something a lot more important than your dreams that does.**

And that is your Unstoppable.

Your Unstoppable isn't a dream. Dreams come and go.[106] They're shattered by circumstances, growing up, and/or having children. Your Unstoppable is bigger than your dreams because it can never be stopped, outgrown, or spit-up on.

The key to discovering your Unstoppable isn't looking at what you want to do, but rather why you want to do it.

You want to be an astronaut. Great. WHY? Being an astronaut is just ONE way to accomplish the thing you truly want: to get drunk on the moon. A lot of people don't know this but that was the Unstoppable that drove my dear friend, client, fellow playboy billionaire, and ally in the

---

[106] Not unlike "wet dreams" which cum and go.

battle to beat artificial intelligence, Elon Musk to invent SpaceX.[107]

Sometimes a limited scope of our future can make us believe there is only one way to get what we want, but when we take a step back and see that what we're after is actually underneath what we thought our dreams were, THAT'S where you'll find your Unstoppable. Dreams will come and go, but your Unstoppable is with you for life.[108]

Look at every dream you've ever had. Why did you have that dream? What would accomplishing that dream actually give you? For example: Joseph and the Amazing Technicolor Dreamcoat dreamed of being bound, gagged, and sold into slavery by his brothers and eventually becoming Pharaoh's right hand man. But what that actually gave him was an opportunity to embarrass his brothers in front of his father. Unstoppable!

---

107 And his lesser known venture, a potent space grain alcohol called "Moonshine."

108 It's the HPV of driving forces.

Unrealized Dream	What It Would Actually Give Me
Example: Become A Rock Star	*Free hotel rooms for life*

Look deeper. **Every dream you've had has been born from your Unstoppable.**[109] What's underneath your dreams? What do you TRULY want to get from these accomplishments?

Now, take it one step further. Once you get what your dream would give you, what do you get the opportunity to give to others? **How would the world benefit from your success?**

Now, take it one step even further! **Who does that make you to the world?**

And ONE MORE STEP FURTHER! What kind of business, branding and merchandising opportunities exist for that you?

---

109 Even that weird one.

I explore that more in my business seminar Money Business Superstars which you can pre-sign up for now at www.DaleThorhammer.com, but for now let's take it one step back.

THAT. That right there. That's your Unstoppable. Write it down.

My Unstoppable is being ______________________________

I told you I'd find it.

Now that you've discovered your Unstoppable, you're starting to be able to see the unlimited possibilities that can and will bring you to it - AND that you're already there in this very moment.[110]

It might not feel like you're there yet,[111] but that's because you were looking at what you thought was the path, not the destination. Now that you're tuned in to what you want, you'll see it's going to start to flood into your life tenfold.

You didn't even really know where you were trying to get to before and you were complaining that you weren't there!

---

110 Congratulations on being in the moment!

111 Remember, feelings are just lies your ego tells you to keep you from leaving it.

We've just replaced your gas with rocket fuel![112] And you're ready to blast off into success and fulfillment. But before we do that, we need to more clearly define what success looks like for you, which I will do for you in this next chapter.

[112] And we've replaced your engine with a rocket engine.

SUCCESS AND HOW IT IS YOU

At its core, this book is about success, however you define it.[113]

But before you define it for yourself, let me define it for you and save you some time.[114] After all, having other people do things for you is one of the most crucial traits of being a powerful person.[115]

This is why I'm going to let someone else define success for me, so I don't have to.

"Started from the bottom now we here."
- My dear friend, client, and Degrassi alumnus, Drake[116]

That's right! Success is here! You're already successful and you didn't even know it.

---

113 Don't yet. I'm going somewhere with this.
114 See? I told you I was going somewhere with this.
115 This paragraph was typed by my assistant. It literally took me no time at all.
116 Whom I taught to overcome playing a character in a wheelchair by encouraging him to act like he can walk again.

We set our own standards for success, so why are you making it so hard? Make success easier to reach and you will feel more successful.

Look at how quickly you're going through this book!

That's because I made the font big so you burn through pages quicker.

Look!

Congratulations!

That took no time at all.

You just read three pages!

The problem most people face when they're feeling unsuccessful is that they're not matching up to where they want to be. If you want to be on a very successful show on NBC, but instead you're slumming it on basic cable, you're going to feel unsuccessful.

It's time to lower that bar![117]

In other words, if you don't feel successful in this very moment, it's because your standards for yourself are too high.

Make success easier to reach and you will feel more successful.

[117] QVC, I'm ready!

Why feel successful? Feeling successful is the gateway to actual success. How can you build upon what's not there? You can't! I learned this the hard way when I discovered one of my many income properties doesn't exist because it couldn't be built as there was no land. What did I do? I made land and built on that. And now, Floating Heights is the most profitable building in all of South South Miami Beach.[118]

If you want to feel successful, start defining success by where you are. Do you have a job? No? Lower. Did you eat this morning? No? EVEN LOWER. Are you breathing in this moment? YES! Success![119]

It's safe to say that the majority of people who have ever existed are NOT breathing in this moment. You, right now, are doing better than John Lennon, Abraham Lincoln, and Salvador Dali put together![120] CELEBRATE!

Sure, maybe they created movements, changed societies, and/or drew clocks funny, but you're breathing and they're not, and that makes you much more successful in this moment than any of them. You can't argue with that.[121]

---

[118] 360-degree oceanfront views!

[119] If you are not breathing, call 911 and ask them to support you in bettering your life by helping it to continue.

[120] Do not put John Lennon, Abraham Lincoln, and Salvador Dali together. That way lies madness.

[121] This is a book. You can try, but this has already been printed and therefore won't change its mind.

The key to feeling successful is constant and premature celebration. The more you celebrate the little things and what you've already done to get to where you are, the cooler people will think you are and the more stuff they will bring into your life.[122]

Don't get me wrong,[123] having goals is important. In fact, accomplishment is one of the feelings humans need most frequently in order to live a fulfilling life. This is why I always set my goals impossibly low. And look at me now! I look great.

---

[122] "Look at that person breathing! I want to hang out with someone like that!"

[123] Ever.

Me, Now

LOW GOALS, HIGH ACHIEVEMENT

I wanted to write this book in order to change the lives of billions of people.[124] Quite a grandiose goal, isn't it? If I looked at it that way every day, would I have ever written it? Yes. But that's because I've wired my brain toward achieving the impossible.[125] However, in order to make the impossible manageable, I created smaller "mini-goals" to write at least one life-changing power sentence every day to keep me accomplishing my goals at a rate that I find acceptable: all the time.

Granted, most days I wrote way more than one life-changing power sentence, and then I got to celebrate my accomplishments doubly because I not only accomplished my goal, I DECIMATED IT!

This book was written over a period of 6 years and it's the most life-changing, powerful book that you'll ever be reading right now.

---

124 I only measure in billions.

125 Did that seem impossible at the time? Yes.

I am currently working toward my goal of learning alchemy through process of elimination by discovering at least one way to NOT turn something into gold every week. I'm crushing it.

Make your goals attainable, measurable, and without a ceiling.[126] That sounds doable. And doable is the only way I set my goals and live my life. The easiest goals to accomplish are ones that are easily accomplishable.

---

126 Like a great convertible or a bad Airbnb.

THERE IS NO "I" IN TEAM – THERE'S A "ME"[127]

If you're one of those people who has been reading this book and thinking that it sounds nice but coming up with excuses for how this doesn't apply to you, don't worry. You're in the right place.[128]

You might be of the belief that you need more than what you have and who you are to get to where you want to be.

What a cruel joke it would be to give someone a passion or a desire that they could never amount to. Everything you want in your life, you are capable of getting. You were given this life because you're strong enough to live it. Generally speaking, if you weren't capable then you wouldn't want it. And I don't speak in generalities, I speak in Universal Truths.[129]

The mere fact that you desire something means that you have the capability inside of you to go and get it. All you need is within you now.[130] It's living in your desire and your gut - along with a lot of healthy bacteria.

---

127 Also "Tea"

128 Look around. Wherever you are is correct. Celebrate!

129 Universally speaking.

130 Assuming you have already read this book.

Your desire is your driving force toward accomplishment, which is why we can't necessarily accomplish the things others want us to do. **We have to want it for ourselves.** This alone makes me a terrible low level employee. I've always known that I'd rather work toward my dreams than have someone else pay me to work toward theirs. This is why I manifested myself getting fired from Blockbuster Video.[131] So, this idea that you need more than you have is just bullshit, distracting, and counterproductive,[132] and as its boss it's your job to fire it.[133]

If you feel lacking, give yourself what you want. **Whatever you feel you need, you have to give. If you can give it to yourself, other people will sense that you don't need them and you'll find they're more attracted to you than ever.** The first law of attraction is that people are attracted to that which doesn't nag them for shit. As your desperation fades away, and self-sufficiency and self care take over its lease in your psyche, you'll find you're much more capable than you thought you were.

Once you realize the things you need and can give to yourself, you'll discover they start to show up more and more in your life. This is also known as manifestation. In the next chapter I'm going to show you how to master this

---

131 I also manifested them going out of business, so who's still breathing now?

132 The worst kind of productive.

133 Without severance.

skill to bring ANYTHING and EVERYTHING you've wanted into your life quicker and easier than you ever thought possible.

I know, those are some bold promises, but fortune favors the bold, and I've had many articles written about me in Fortune Magazine.

PART THREE
CREATING YOUR FUTURE

Look how far you've come! *So* far![134]

We've eliminated all of life's problems, erased your past, and shown you that you're capable and deserving of having anything you want in the world. And that was just the first ⅔ of this book. You're getting so much value for what you paid.[135]

From here on out, you're going to be stepping into the future that you want. It's so close you can smell it, especially if you bought the deluxe version of this book where this page has a scratch and sniff with the scent of dreams.[136]

---

[134] Remember when you were only on page 1? And think about how much further you'll have come once you finish this book.

[135] If you feel like you're getting more value than you paid for, please Venmo @DaleThorhammer the remaining balance to maintain the proper energy exchange.

[136] Which is a combination of waffle-cones, leather, and jasmine.

CREATION PROCESS

The word "meditation" itself is enough to bring some people to a snoring halt. And I get it, meditation involves tremendous inner stillness which is boring and the opposite of moving forward, which we've established is the only direction I move.[137]

That's why right now I'm going to guide you through my Creation Process™. This is in no way a boring meditation and, in fact, is completely different.[138] If at any point you feel relaxed, calm, or full of inner peace - remind yourself that this isn't a meditation, so it's totally normal to have those experiences.

First, make sure you are in an uncomfortable position with your legs crossed and your back straight. During my time spent in India studying consciousness, all of the most conscious and enlightened teachers were sitting in very uncomfortable positions for hours. Sitting uncomfortably is

---

137 Lateral moves are the gateway to going backwards.

138 And legally trademarked.

one of the shortcuts to enlightenment that hasn't yet made its way into the western world.[139]

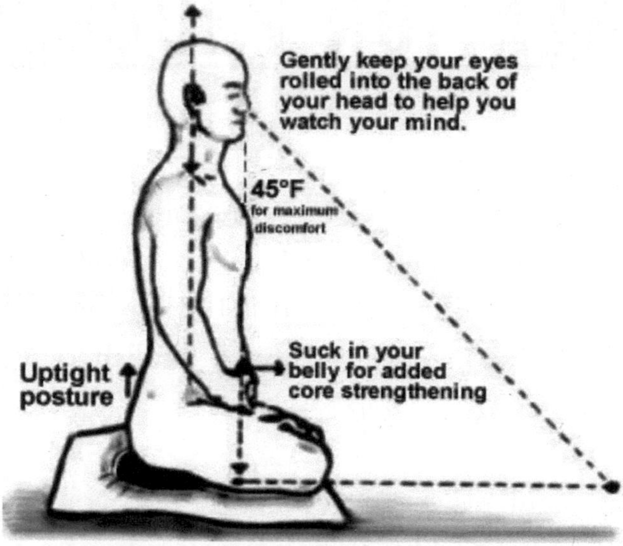

Preferred Uncomfortable Meditation Position

This process is best done in a quiet place, but if you don't have a quiet place it can also be done intermittently interrupted by noisy roommates, neighbors, animals, small children, or passing cars.[140] If you would like some soothing music, you can access a complimentary audio track at www.StopStoppingTheUnstoppable.com/SoothingAudio. If you're not by a device that can play audio, you can easily create your own by banging gongs, humming to yourself,

[139] La-Z-Boys are the ultimate enemy of inner peace and core strength.

[140] In fact, it's more powerful if you're being disturbed by real world distractions that remind you of all your looming responsibilities.

and asking a stranger to take deep calming breaths into your ear.

Once you're in your preferred and primed Process Space™, take a deep breath and close your eyes.

Close your eyes.

Take a deep breath. And close your eyes.

Feel your body. Don't open your eyes.

How are you reading this? Your eyes are supposed to be closed. Close your eyes.

Feel your eyes, feel their closed-ness.

Take a deep breath, down into the ground. Through the floor. Keep breathing in.

And breathe it down. Down into the center of the earth. Into the liquid hot core of the earth.

And breathe out, bringing that energy up into your body. That's yours now. We'll figure out how you can pay me for it later.

Picture your life as it is today. In this present moment. Find something that you can be grateful for that already exists.

You don't have to do anything to have it, it's there for you already. Be grateful for it.

Now, I want you to go back to a moment in your life where everything felt okay. Everything was fine, you didn't have to do anything or be anyone else, you were great as you are. See that version of you. Nod at them.

Go ten years into the future. See your life the way you want it. Your house, your job, your relationship. See that future you. Feel it as if it's real. Look around at your life and really take it in as if it's happening. Feel it happening. Feel it having had already happened. Do you have a two story house with a water slide connecting the top and bottom floor? Yeah, you do. It's your life. This is yours. See who you are, who is the you that made all this happen, who did you have to be? That is you. Own it. Feel that you in your body right now.

Now, think of something else. It can be anything you want. Actually, you know what? Make it a dinosaur. Think of a dinosaur. What color is the dinosaur? Is it purple? Make it orange. An orange dinosaur. Picture that dinosaur. Clear as day, right in front of you. And when that dinosaur in front of you feels so real, you can see it so clearly and you know it's there, I want you to turn the page…

One more…

Look at what you created! Look at how powerful you are. If you had envisioned a green monster truck, that's what you would have seen, but you didn't. You imagined an orange dinosaur, and it appeared because you're powerful. And just as you created this dinosaur in front of you now, so too did you create the future that you envisioned. It's there waiting for you.[141]

Now all you have to do is go and get it!

[141] Hello!

WORKSHEET

You've now seen your future and felt it as if it were real. Virtual Reality has nothing on Reality Reality.[142] Write down the future that you saw. Write it as if it's currently happening right in front of you:

142 One of my many companies is developing a new Reality Reality headset that you can wear to look around at the world you actually live in. It's very realistic and will be very successful. I've emboldened my publishers to include a free pair for you on the next page.

Instructions: cut out headset and look through eyepiece to see reality in stunning clarity

MANIFESTATION (AND WOMANIFESTATION)

If you're looking at your current life and wondering where all the good parts you just saw are, then you're going to enjoy this chapter. I'm going to teach you how to bring anything you want into your life quicker and bigger than you ever thought was possible. I call it *BIG*-ing where you wish for a better life and overnight turn into a striking 32 year old Tom Hanks.

I have to warn you,[143] these concepts I'm about to introduce you to might make you uncomfortable[144] because they're going to challenge what you already believe. So, before we get into it, let me turn you against those old beliefs by reminding you that your current set of beliefs is what got you into this mindset of suffering and stagnation in the first place. It hasn't been doing you any favors and hardly contributes its fair share of the rent.[145]

---

[143] Legally

[144] Like the concept of an actually 12-year-old Tom Hanks having sex with Elizabeth Perkins.

[145] Its fair share is "all of it."

In fact, without those beliefs you wouldn't even need this chapter because you'd already be doing what I'm about to tell you. Your beliefs are wasting your time! If you didn't have those beliefs you could be on the next chapter already!

Now that you're skeptical of your previous thoughts and beliefs, we're going to stand on either side of you and both call your name like you would to a dog. Whoever you go to will be your rightful owner. Here's the question you need to ask yourself: Do you own your beliefs, or do your beliefs own you?[146]

So why do you not have the things you want in life already? Simple:

We attract what we're attracting.

You've got to feel it to get it. Got it?

It's the law of attraction.[147]

The law of attraction states that the more attractive you are, the easier it is to get what you want. The more attractive you are, the more things people will straight up give you.

So, how do you get more attractive? Simple. Attractive people understand this one clear principle: look good.

---

[146] It should be noted that beliefs tend to have the people that they own spayed and/or neutered. Just saying.

[147] Enforced in all fifty Emotional States.

Whether you're wearing fashionable large brimmed hats,[148] prayer beads, or just a smile, it's important to look good.[149]

But what if you can't afford prayer beads, smiles, or fashionable flower crowns?[150]

You're going to have to learn how to look good on the inside. This is where the radical thinking comes in.

We are beings of vibrational energy, and whatever level we are vibrating at decides what shows up in our lives. If you experience a lot of negativity, you're vibrating at a negative level. If you are being attacked by a shark it's because you are attracting the shark by vibrating at a chum level.[151]

Everything you have in your life, both good and bad, you've called to yourself through vibrational energy. You can blame external circumstances all you want, but the truth of the matter is that you did this.

Now, I'm not saying everything bad that's happened to you in your life is your fault. I'm saying it's your responsibility.

---

148 At the time of writing this, large hats are VERY fashionable.

149 Naked smiling people are very good looking.

150 Large brimmed hats are out, everyone is wearing flower crowns now.

151 If you are *currently* being attacked by a shark, don't worry. You're in the right place. Keep reading this book to learn to recalibrate your vibrational level to become someone who would punch a shark in the face.

If someone breaks into my house and robs me blind, it wasn't my fault. But it WAS my responsibility to ensure that my dog Bernard wasn't tied up so when that asswipe broke into my house he became dog food. Rest assured, Bernard now has a much longer chain and has since been conditioned to have a Pavlovian thirst for intruder blood.

In taking responsibility for what happened, I was able to grow and learn in order to create a new future for myself where I'm invulnerable to home invasions. In fact, Bernard and I invite anyone reading this right now to try.

If you focus on what the things that you want look like, you're going to be constantly comparing that imaginary future to what you currently have. Comparison comes from a mindset of lacking.

Stop looking at how you want your future to *look*, and start concentrating on how you want your future to *feel*. Feelings, while not real, are powerful manifestation tools when you learn to take the control of them away from your ego.[152]

Forget "Fake it 'til you make it."- FEEL IT 'til you REAL IT!

---

[152] Ego abused its feelings privileges and is on a timeout until it learns to stop making everything about itself.

I can't tell you how many times I've heard someone say, "Fake it til you make it" - because whenever someone says something inauthentic, I black out.

Don't fake it 'til you make it. **Feel it til you real it.**

Faking it until you make it is bullshit because that makes you a liar. Lying will only get you so far.

However, there's no more powerful source of energy than true delusion.

People say, "Dale, I can't do that. I can't FEEL something that I'm not am."

If you truly believe something, no matter how absurd, then no one can tell you otherwise.

You can spend your life feeling out of place and repeating "fake it til you make it" - terrified of being found out. That doesn't sound like a powerful life to me and I know powerful lives - I'm living one right now.

Find the feeling you're after - the feeling of that high-paying job, the feeling of that new relationship, the feeling of finishing that marathon.

You know who finishes marathons? Marathon runners. Once you *feel* like a marathon runner, you'll be running that marathon in no time. You know what people who fake being marathon runners wind up being? Dehydrated.

Feel it. Act it. Do it.

Some people say, "But Dale, I don't know how to feel like a marathon runner." Yes you do. If you didn't know how to feel it, you wouldn't know how to want it. If you didn't know what it feels like, then what are you wanting? You know what you want it to feel like. So go feel that.

Feel how you want your future to feel and it will raise your vibrational energy and immediately start to attract your future to you. When you change how and what you feel on the inside, your outside can't help but follow suit and make you more attractive on the outside as well.[153]

Feel it til you real it.

---

[153] Your outsides are spineless and will do whatever your insides say, because your spine is on the inside.

DISCOVERING THE BETTER YOU

During the Creation Process you got to see and feel your fulfilled, Unstoppable life. Who would you need to be in order to accomplish that? What type of person was able to achieve your dreams?

This person might look different from who you think you are - or who your past life has told you that you are. But remember what we said about the past[154]- divorce your story.

So if you don't think you're capable of being that person who could achieve your dreams so hard, be a different person.

Try to be me. And by failing to be me, you'll be a better you.

Don't be who you think you are, be who ***I*** think you are.

---

154 Figuratively speaking. Because, remember, I only look forward.

WORKSHEET

Based on who you saw in your future, know that that's who I see you as. I want you to make a list of all the qualities and characteristics that I see in you and KNOW you to be.

WHO DOES DALE THINK I AM?

INSTALLING THE NEW YOU

You're doing great! I knew I could get you there.

Now that you see the truth about who you actually are,[155] you want to make sure you[156] are constantly able to access this real, powerful you.[157]

In order for you to fully accept who I think you are as the truth, we'll need to work together to override the old you that's been driving you further into the woods searching for what's been right under your nose the entire time. *That* you still serves a purpose, sure, but we've seen what happens when it's at the steering wheel and let's be honest, it's probably better as a passenger.[158]

---

155 Me.
156 Me.
157 Me.
158 Don't let it touch the radio.

How do you make sure that this new you sticks? Declare it. Lie to yourself out loud until you believe yourself out quiet.

Look at the "Who Does Dale Think I Am" worksheet on the previous page and declare out loud that you ARE those things.

"I AM _______________!"

Declare it strong, into a mirror, and loud enough that your neighbors will think you're overcompensating.

Do this over and over again until you are hoarse and uncomfortable, and then do it five more times.[159] There's no limit to the amount of noise complaints you can get to make this work.[160]

Look at yourself. Feel how powerful you are from this place. What's possible from here? ANYTHING! EVERYTHING!

Give yourself a new name from this place.

My name is Dale "Fucking Unstoppable" Thorhammer. I declared that and it's true.[161] The same goes for you. Who cares what your old name was? Was it John? Was it Emily? Was it Kal-El Cage? Whatever it was - that's not you. That's something your parents told you that you were and

---

[159] And then five more times.

[160] This is not a legal opinion. Consult local statutes and regulations.

[161] According to my driver's license.

you believed them. What else did your parents tell you? Probably a lot of things to keep you safe, protected, and in line.

How long are you going to let your parents keep making your decisions for you? Only *you* know what's best for you. Everyone else is just taking best guesses. And best guesses are only good for losing people millions of dollars on Who Wants To Be A Millionaire. Lucky for you, you're phoning a friend, and that friend is YOU![162]

It's time for the new you to take over! You're done living a safe, protected, and "in line" life! You've got your Unstoppable to stop stopping!

Give yourself a name, a pose, or any signal that can train your body and mind to know that this is who you are now. And if you ever forget it, you call yourself forward.

Just like my dear friend, client, and overt Caucasian, Marshall Mathers declared himself "Eminem" to overcome societal barriers and achieve his dream of becoming a successful entrepreneur and single father.

---

[162] ME!

DECLARE IT!

HI, MY NAME IS ____________________

MY NAME IS _____________________

MY NAME IS (CHICKA CHICKA) ____________

How do you make a dog yours? You give it a name and you teach it to come when you call it.[163]

You're a dog and you're going to make yourself come![164]

---

[163] And how to read.

[164] Good dog!

DECLARATIONS, COMMITMENT, AND ACTION

Now that you've declared your new self, it's time to look upon what you want to create with your new, capable eyes.

It's time to commit to your future, to step into it with a powerful declaration. **Fear of commitment is nothing compared to a fear of an unfulfilled life.**[165] Thinking about your future won't bring your future to you. You have to go out and get it. And the only way to go out and get something is to take action toward it.

Make a list of goals for your future. You can reference the worksheet after the Creative Process™ for ideas.

Remember: it's not plagiarism if you're stealing from yourself.[166] Write them as if they are happening:

---

165 Outscare yourself into action!

166 Unless you're super litigious.

The next year:

1. I am...
2.
3.
4.
5.

The next 5 years

1. I am...
2.
3.
4.
5.

The next 10 years

1. I am...
2.
3.
4.
5.

The next 100 years[167]

1. I am...
2.
3.
4.
5.

---

[167] If you don't think you're going to be alive 100 years from now, make "being alive" your first 100-year goal.

Make a list of actions small and large[168] that you can take now or in the future toward bringing these goals into your reality. And once your goals become reality, they are no longer goals, they are parts of your life that you get to take for granted so you can pine after something new. Keep accomplishing so that you can keep trying to accomplish.

Goal	Action

[168] Or as I call them "Actions" and "Actions"

BE YOUR UNSTOPPABLE

"You down with OPP? Yeah, you know me."
- My dear friends, clients, and notorious adulterers, Naughty By Nature

You see where you want to go, you know WHO you have to be to get there…

Now all you need is a worthy adversary. That's right! An opponent.[169] If life gave you everything you wanted when you asked for it you'd never have any fun. You'd be like one of those miserable rich kids of Instagram who keep buying boats to post online but never learn the joys of selling a boat and buying a plane instead.[170]

The quality of your life is dictated by the quality of the forces opposing you. The greater opposition you face, the more heroic you get to be. Like Superman, who has an incredible quality of life due to overcoming the biggest oppositional force of all - gravity.[171] If it weren't for gravity, you would be flying right now. How powerful of a life would that be?

---

169 Or Fun-pponent.
170 First joy: Mile-High Club is instantly more attainable.
171 Superman's other greatest opponent: growing up without a father.

Now that you're your Unstoppable You, you're ready for obstacles worthy of your legacy.

Don't worry, life is going to throw shit at you.[172] Unrelentingly and constantly! But you're ready for it because you've been eating shit for years. You now know if there's one way to your goal then there's two ways to your goal. And if there are two ways to your goal, then there are three ways to your goal. And if there are three ways to your goal then there are UNLIMITED WAYS TO YOUR GOAL.

So when life throws you a block, you're going to know to look for:

Other
Possible
Possibilities

Nothing can stop you. You are Unstoppable. You are DOWN with OPP![173] You will find new and creative ways to get to what you want. You've got all the tools now. You know who you are, you know what you're up to, and no one can tell you otherwise.

---

[172] Much like zoo animals.
[173] Yeah, I know you![1]
[1]Me.

No one, that is, except for… yourself. This is why in this next chapter I'm going to show you the final step to ensure that you never stop stop stopping your Unstoppable.

NEVER STOP STOP STOPPING THE UNSTOPPABLE

The only thing that can stop you at this point is the most dangerous emotion known to mankind:

SHAME.

Shame will stop you dead in your tracks.[174] It will make you doubt yourself. It will make you question everything that you're up to.

Shame sneaks up on you in the form of thoughts.[175] The voice that tells you you aren't good enough, or you're unsure, or you don't deserve what you want.[176] It's the thought that tells you that you shouldn't have eaten that cake, or that everyone in the office hates you, or that you should have waited for your co-worker John to at least blow out his candles before you ate his cake.

---

[174] So will being "hangry"

[175] It knew I was going to say that.

[176] Do you want another copy of this book? You deserve it.

Time spent in shame is time better spent doing things better NOW.

Identify shame. See it as it happens. Say "I see you shame. You're not going to get me. I have a very particular set of skills that make me a nightmare for emotions like you." I call this Liam Neeson-ing, because of how he taught his son not to be embarrassed in *Love, Actually*.[177]

Descarte said, "I think, therefore I am."

Well, Dale Thorhammer says, "I don't think, therefore I am better!"

Shame doesn't exist outside of thoughts. So stop thinking!

Thinking is not enough anymore. Thinking is what got you stuck. Stop thinking and just be. You're a human being, not a human thinking.

Thinking will always be present as long as you have a functioning brain. And to be honest, the lobotomy technology just isn't there yet so the most you can do is be aware.

---

[177] Which is different from my business/finance strategy of Liam Neeson-ing where you make a list of all the assets you want to save.

And you know what? You're going to slip up. You're not going to win every battle. And that's okay, because in the next chapter I'm going to show you how to win even when you lose.[178]

[178] Like an emotional Electoral College.

LOVE YOURSELF

People can tend to beat the hell out of themselves when they slip up.

If you go off your diet, SCREW IT! PASS ME THE OREOS™ !

If you mess up at work, how long do you spend punishing yourself for that mistake? That's valuable time that could be used not making future mistakes.

And then how often do you punish yourself for punishing yourself because you should know better?

That's shame. That's shame sneaking in and pulling you down into the sewer. It's like the monster from Stephen King's *IT*.[179]

But here's how you can beat it: by loving yourself.[180]

---

[179] The real monster was the length of that book.

[180] Note: "beating it" is also a great way to love yourself.

Can you love yourself? With all of your "mistakes" and "flaws"?[181] If you can love yourself in the face of everything you are, everything you do "wrong,"[182] you're going to improve your Shame Recovery Rate™[183] tenfold.

Maybe you're sad and people are telling you to not be sad and you feel sadder that you're sad and making people sad that you're sad.

Be freaking sad!

Are you mad? SCREW IT! BE FREAKING MAD! It's okay to be mad!

All of these emotions are okay to have! Don't let other people tell you who to be! Stop looking outside of yourself for answers because YOU already know. You're just looking for external confirmation. You don't need it. You've got it all inside of you.[184] Only YOU know what's truly right for YOU.

Just love yourself while you do it.

---

[181] Or as I call them "Learn-speriences"™ and "Character Quirks"™. Example: My friend Andy has this Character Quirk where he sociopathically lies when he's scared.

[182] Alternatively correct

[183] To find your Shame Recovery Rate™, take the number of minutes between making your mistake and being able to forgive yourself for it and divide that by the number of things you could've accomplished in that amount of time.

[184] And in this book.

When's the last time you said "I love myself"? Better yet, when's the last time you yelled "I love myself!"?[185]

Do it now. Loudly and without pause.

Say it out loud! It doesn't matter if it's true. It's like I told my dear friend, client, and famous Dana Carvey impressionist, Dana Carvey: the first step to loving yourself is lying about it out loud.

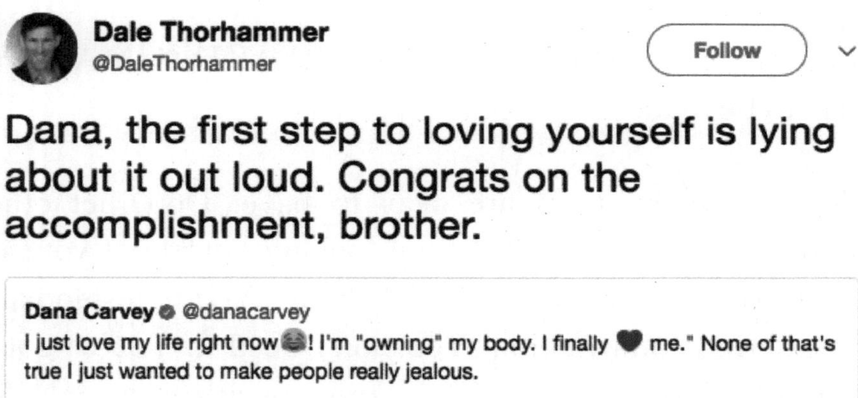
Dale Thorhammer
@DaleThorhammer
Follow

Dana, the first step to loving yourself is lying about it out loud. Congrats on the accomplishment, brother.

Dana Carvey @danacarvey
I just love my life right now😂! I'm "owning" my body. I finally 🖤 me." None of that's true I just wanted to make people really jealous.

Keep saying it. Keep searching in yourself for anything and everything that you don't want to love and give it a ton of love! Love yourself wholly. Love yourself completely. Love every inch of yourself, especially the parts that are weird and unsightly - the parts that you don't want to love - love them the most!

---

[185] I did just now as I wrote this. And even as I'm being escorted out of this cafe, I'm in deep, deep love with myself.

Because the only way to Stop Stopping The Unstoppable is when you can learn to

LOVE LOVING THE UNLOVABLE

FUCKING ALL THIS UP

You're almost done! Look at you, finishing something you started. I personally don't believe in finishing things because that would mean that things have ends. As we all know,[186] life is a constant work in progress and there is no end. Not even death. Just ask Steve Jobs.[187]

But now that you have all the knowledge that was previously on these pages now forever held hostage inside your brain creating a sort of informational munchausen syndrome,[188] you're set for life to be perfect forever, correct?

Kind of. And by "kind of" of course I mean "absolutely not." You're going to fail. But here's the Dale Thorhammer spin - you're going to look forward to failing.

We've all heard the phrase "fail forward." Well, failing forward is bullshit.

Don't fail forward, Fuck UP!

---

186 Me all know.

187 This requires knowing that Steve had his consciousness uploaded into Siri.

188 This is how I refer to "reading."

Every time you Fuck UP is an opportunity for you to learn, grow, and yell "FUCK" out loud - a beloved pastime of successful people and bad golfers.[189]

Think about it, as humans one of our main driving factors is reproduction - fucking, and which direction are you doing it in? UPWARDS! The direction you want to be moving!

Reproduce upwards and FUCK UP!

Don't fear the fuck up, look forward to the fuck up- because if you're not fucking up, then you're fucking up, and that's fucked up.

---

[189] But not of successful golfers and bad people

PART 4
WHAT'S NEXT?

Now that your life is changed and everything you've ever wanted is falling into place, it is your duty to the Universe to point this out to other people and recommend ways that they can change their life in the most obnoxious and all-knowing way possible.[190]

Don't hesitate. Even if you feel like you don't know it all, you know me and I know it all. So by the transitive property of knowledge, you too know it all.

Most people would tell you that this transformation is a muscle, and in order to maintain this new life and state of self-love you should practice it and get a coach to help keep you on track and on your A-Game.[191]

---

[190] And buy them several copies of this book. Lending them this one would only deny them the opportunity to keep it.

[191] And your B and C game. Always be on all your games.

Why *Get* A Life Coach When You Can *Be* A Life Coach?

If you're really looking to continue creating a life you love and pursuing your Unstoppable, it's time to get UNREASONABLE. After all, a reasonable life is fine, but an unreasonable life is impossible to argue with.

Become a life coach.

Coaches make just as much as therapists but without all that training that gets in the way of true communication. While a therapist might diagnose someone as a narcissistic recluse with delusions of grandeur, you can see them for what they truly are: an entrepreneur.

A coach doesn't have a degree to bog down what should be person-to-inspiring-person communication. Why should you take life advice from a doctor when you're not a doctor? You're a regular person just like them, but who has read this book and got it all figured out.

Unlike a therapist, a success coach isn't bound by legal non-disclosures and is able to share their client's progress with the world so people know the difference they're making and how good they are as a coach. This is important. Therapists have something called doctor-patient confidentiality that prohibits them from talking about all the weird stuff their clients are into and therefore limits the amount of people who can see and FEEL their clients' progress.

You might be saying, "Dale, I don't have my life together, I can't be a life coach for others." That doesn't matter. In fact, which part of you is saying "I can't"?

Certainly not the part of you that can. And it's the part of you that can that I want to talk to.

Coaches range in varying degrees of education. Some of the best coaches I know (and work with) simply *decided* that they wanted to be life coaches. That's the first, most important, and sometimes[192] only step to becoming a life coach.

Once you've declared yourself a coach, you're ready to start accepting clients and change the world one life at a time.[193] There are many books out there that I've written that can and should inspire you to be a life coach yourself. Once you know the information and skills of how to achieve happiness and fulfillment, it's on you to pass it on with certainty to all

---

192 Always.

193 Because that's how many people will be watching your webinar.

souls you interact with in order to continue the expansion of global consciousness - even if you yourself aren't living by these principles.

"A woke society begets awokenness.
And being woke is the only way to realize how asleep you've always been."
- my dear friend, client, and me, Dale Thorhammer

If you're interested in getting a life coach, or becoming a life coach, you can reach out to me directly on Facebook[194] and we will train you in the art of transformation so you can start your Facebook Live seminars as soon as possible.

Buy this book for a friend so I can change their lives the way that you've so graciously let me change yours.[195]

194 http://www.facebook.com/DaleThorhammer
195 By buying this book.

POSTFACE

That's it! You're done! Yes, this book was a quick and easy read. You might be saying to yourself, "Dale, it should be harder than this." But, like I said at the beginning of this book, all you needed to do was buy the book and your life would transform instantaneously. I would do all the work for you. You reading it was just a bonus for you. It's already happening and always has been.

Trust me.

Now go live a powerful life - that I can take credit for.

I've changed your life.

- Dale "Fucking Unstoppable" Thorhammer

ACKNOWLEGEMENTS

This book would not have been possible without the countless teachers and friends that have supported me along the way. I'd like to thank my parents, Corey and Brenda for their unwavering support; my dear friends Jake Maccoby and Andrew Ross-Perry for their contributions to comedy and my life; my friends Ben Rolnik, Trudy Green and Mark Shapiro for their encouragement and belief in Stop Stopping The Unstoppable and me; to Aaron Arnold who did the photography for the cover of this book - and to everyone else who read the manuscript of this book and laughed or scoffed their way through it. And of course, to Dale Thorhammer - I couldn't have done it without him.

ABOUT THE AUTHOR

Ross Everett is a comedian based out of Los Angeles, California. His work has been featured on NBC, Hulu, Sirius XM, and Fox Sports. He can be seen touring around the world with his personal development parody show STOP STOPPING THE UNSTOPPABLE and you can reach him at Ross@TheRossEverett.com or through www.StopStoppingTheUnstoppable.com

You've opened the book the wrong way. Where else in your life are you doing that? Good news, you're one step away from turning your life, and this book, around.